SIKH
FESTIVALS AND TRADITIONS

by Jasneet Kaur

PEBBLE
a capstone imprint

Published by Pebble, an imprint of Capstone
1710 Roe Crest Drive, North Mankato, Minnesota 56003
capstonepub.com

Copyright © 2025 by Capstone. All rights reserved. No part of this publication may
be reproduced in whole or in part, or stored in a retrieval system, or transmitted
in any form or by any means, electronic, mechanical, photocopying, recording, or
otherwise, without written permission of the publisher.

Library of Congress Cataloging-in-Publication Data is available
on the Library of Congress website.
ISBN: 9780756594251 (hardcover)
ISBN: 9780756594305 (paperback)
ISBN: 9780756594299 (ebook PDF)

Summary: Sikh people live all over the world, and they celebrate festivals and special
days in many ways. Discover the traditions, celebrations, and histories behind
Gurpurab, Bandi Chhor Divas, Hola Mohalla, and other important Sikh days.

Editorial Credits
Designer: Dina Her; Media Researcher: Jo Miller; Production Specialist: Tori Abraham

Image Credits
Alamy: Ira Berger, 7, Paul Doyle, 8, World Religions Photo Library, 29; Getty Images:
Dinodia Photo, cover (bottom), Hindustan Times, 19, Malcolm P Chapman, cover
(top), Pacific Press, 15; Shutterstock: Attitude, background (throughout), Nitish
Waila, 13, Peter Newton, 1, reddees, 11, Siddharth Setia, 21, StockGalery, 14,
TamasV, 5, Tingling1, 17, travelview, 23, zixia, 25; SuperStock: Cavan Images, 26

Any additional websites and resources referenced in this book are not maintained,
authorized, or sponsored by Capstone. All product and company names are
trademarks™ or registered® trademarks of their respective holders.

Printed and bound in China. 6098

TABLE OF CONTENTS

Introduction to Sikhism 4

The Birth of the Khalsa 6

Bandi Chhor Divas 12

Gurpurab and Shaheedi Purab........ 16

Hola Mohalla 20

Life Events 22

Glossary 30

Read More 31

Internet Sites..................................... 31

Index 32

About the Author 32

Words in **bold** are in the glossary.

INTRODUCTION TO SIKHISM

Sikhism was founded in Punjab, India. Today, though, Sikhs come from all backgrounds. Sikhism is the fifth-largest religion in the world.

Guru Nanak was the religion's founder. He was born in 1469. There were nine Gurus after Guru Nanak. The last Guru died in 1708. The Gurus taught that we are all one and should have equal rights. The holy scripture is called Guru Granth Sahib Ji. Any Sikh can lead prayers from the holy book.

Sikhs worship in a house of worship called a gurdwara. Afterward, everyone sits on the floor together to eat **Langar**. This shows that everyone is equal.

The holy scripture in a gurdwara

THE BIRTH OF THE KHALSA

In 1699, the tenth Guru created a community of saint-soldiers. He called them the Khalsa. *Khalsa* means "pure." Today, members of the Khalsa follow the Guru Granth Sahib Ji like a guru.

Sikhs are initiated into the group for life. Female members take the last name Kaur. Men use the last name Singh. Giving everyone the same name shows that everyone is equal.

A woman reads the Guru Granth Sahib Ji.

Initiated Sikhs are easily recognized by their five articles of faith.

Members of the Khalsa have a special uniform with a turban called a dastaar. Women can also wear turbans if they choose. There are five articles of faith that they wear at all times.

Each article has its own special meaning. Uncut hair signifies spirituality. An iron or steel bracelet reminds them to do good deeds. A sword tells them to stand up for justice. A wooden comb prompts them to be clean. Undershorts are symbols of self-discipline.

Today, the birth of the Khalsa is celebrated during a spring festival called Vaisakhi. It usually takes place on April 13 or 14. Families visit their local gurdwara. Many wear blue and orange, the colors of the Khalsa.

Most gurdwaras hold a fair with sweets, games for kids, and **Punjabi** foods like jalebi, a sweet spiral-shaped treat. Sikh martial arts called gatka are demonstrated. There is also a special initiation ceremony for anyone ready to join the Khalsa.

Sikhs do martial arts to celebrate Vaisakhi.

BANDI CHHOR DIVAS

Sikhs light lamps for Bandi Chhor Divas in October or November. This is a day of liberation.

In 1617, India's Emperor Jahangir did not like how popular Sikhism was becoming. He threw the sixth Guru, Guru Hargobind, in jail.

When the Guru was released two years later, he insisted that 52 innocent kings be freed as well. Then he returned to the city of Amritsar. Sikhs celebrated his return by lighting bright clay lamps.

Fireworks are set off near the historic Golden Temple in Amritsar to celebrate Bandi Chhor Divas every year.

Diya lights use oil, which gives their flames a warm glow.

Today, many Sikhs around the world decorate the outside of their houses and gurdwaras with lights for Bandi Chhor Divas. Some also light candles and special lamps called diyas inside their houses. Many families make special meals and sweets.

Bandi Chhor Divas is a day to think of others. Sikhs celebrate this day with their community. In India, neighborhood parades called Nagar **Kirtan** take place. People gather to sing hymns that celebrate their faith.

Nagar Kirtan are part of some Sikh celebrations.

GURPURAB AND SHAHEEDI PURAB

Gurpurab are birthday celebrations for the Gurus. The Gurpurab for the first Guru is the largest. It takes place in November. It begins with an early morning parade called Prabhat Pheri. Sikhs sing Kirtan while walking in their neighborhood.

Later, Sikhs meet at the gurdwara. They sing hymns and tell stories related to Guru Nanak's life and teaching. Then Langar is enjoyed.

Special Gurpurab programs are held for children at gurdwaras. Families who can't go to a gurdwara might pray at home or make a special sweet dish called **parshaad**.

All gurdwaras have a Langar hall, or community kitchen. Everyone is welcome.

The birth of a Guru is not the only way to celebrate Sikhism's founders. Their sacrifices are remembered as well.

The fifth Guru, Guru Arjan, and the ninth Guru, Guru Tegh Bahadur, were **martyrs**. They sacrificed their lives for fairness and freedom of religion for all people. The days remembering these martyrs are called Shaheedi Purab.

A sweet drink made with milk, water, and rose syrup called chhabeel keeps people cool during Shaheedi Purab.

HOLA MOHALLA

Hola Mohalla is a three-day celebration in March. It was started by the tenth Guru, Guru Gobind Singh, in 1701. The biggest event is held in the holy city of Anandpur Sahib in India. Prayers, poetry contests, and Kirtan are all part of the festivities.

Warriors called Nihang Singhs wear blue robes and turbans decorated with weapons. Mock battles display their mastery of weapons and gatka. Big parades show off their horseback riding skills.

Horsemanship is an important part of Khalsa tradition.

LIFE EVENTS

Newborn babies receive their names during Janam Sanskaar. At the gurdwara, families listen to Kirtan. A prayer called **Ardaas** asks **Vaheguru** to bless the new baby with good health.

After Ardaas, a **Hukamnama** is read from the holy book. The Guru Granth Sahib is opened at random. The hymn on that page is the lesson for the day. The family chooses the baby's name using the first letter of the hymn.

The Gurus encouraged strong family ties.

Long, uncut hair is part of life as a Khalsa. Adult men, and some women, wear turbans called dastaar. Children use a cloth with four ties called a patka. As they become adults, young Sikhs take part in a special ceremony called Dastaar-Bandi.

During this ceremony, family members pray and help the new adult tie their dastaar. The turban is a special crown from the Gurus. It signifies the teenager's promise to be kind, loving, and fair to everyone.

Boys in a patka (left) and dastaar (right).

Sikh weddings are called "blissful unions."

Marriage ceremonies called Anand Karaj are held at the gurdwara. The bride and the groom sit on the floor in front of the Guru Granth Sahib. While special hymns called laavaan are recited, they walk clockwise around the holy book.

Finally, the couple receives a blessing from the Guru Granth Sahib Ji. Everyone gathers for Langar afterward.

When people die, their bodies are cremated. A full service with prayers and a funeral takes place. Sikhs pray that the soul of their loved one is merged with Vaheguru.

Not every Sikh is born into the religion. **Amrit** Sanchaar is an initiation ceremony. To prepare, people take a bath, wash their hair, and wear their five articles of faith.

Five initiated Sikhs prepare a special drink called Amrit while reciting **Gurbani** prayers. An iron bowl full of clean water is sweetened with special sugar crystals. It is stirred with a double-edged sword called a khanda. Anyone who takes Amrit promises to follow the Guru's teachings.

Amrit means "immortal nectar."

GLOSSARY

Amrit (UM-rit)—a sweet drink made of sugar water that is stirred with a khanda

Ardaas (UR-dahs)—the Sikh prayer that talks about the 10 Gurus and the Sikhs who bravely served their faith; it asks God for blessings to keep everyone well

Gurbani (gur-BAH-nee)—hymns in the Guru Granth Sahib Ji

Hukamnama (HOO-kum-nahh-muh)—the reading of a certain hymn from the Guru Granth Sahib

Kirtan (KEER-tuhn)—special hymns sung from the Guru Granth Sahib often accompanied by different musical instruments

Langar (LUHN-guhr)—a vegetarian meal prepared by volunteers in the gurdwara's kitchen

martyr (MAR-tuhr)—a person who gives their life for a worthy cause

parshaad (pur-SHAHD)—a sweet treat made of wheat flour, sugar, and butter

Punjabi (poon-JAH-bee)—the language and culture of people from Punjab, which is a state in northern India

Vaheguru (VA-hee-goo-roo)—the name Sikhs typically use for God

READ MORE

Bradley, Fleur. *My Life as a Sikh: How the World Worships*. Ann Arbor, MI: Cherry Lake Publishing, 2022.

Demi. *Guru Nanak: First of the Sikhs*. Bloomington, IN: Wisdom Tales, 2021.

Ganeri, Anita. *All Kinds of Beliefs*. New York: Crabtree Publishing Company, 2020.

INTERNET SITES

BBC Bitesize: What Is Sikhism?
bbc.co.uk/bitesize/topics/zsjpyrd/articles/zkjpkmn

Kiddle: Sikhism Facts for Kids
kids.kiddle.co/Sikhism

The Sikh Coalition: About Sikhs
sikhcoalition.org/about-sikhs

INDEX

articles of faith, 8, 9, 28

babies, 22

Bandi Chhor Divas, 12, 13, 14, 15

food, 5, 10, 14, 16, 17, 27

gurdwaras, 5, 10, 14, 16, 17, 22, 27

Gurpurab, 16, 17

Guru Granth Sahib Ji, 4, 6, 7, 22, 27

Guru Nanak, 4, 16

Hola Mohalla, 20

Khalsa, 6, 9, 10, 21, 24

Langar, 5, 16, 17, 27

marriages, 26, 27

martyrs, 18

Nihang Singhs, 20

parades, 15, 16, 20

prayers, 4, 17, 20, 22, 24, 27, 28

Vaisakhi, 10, 11

ABOUT THE AUTHOR

Jasneet Kaur is the author of the children's books *Dream Big, Little Kaur* and *Dream Big, Little Singh*. She is also the founder of a web-based platform for young Sikhs called Curious Khalsa. Jasneet is a mother of two young Kaurs who continue to inspire her. In her spare time, she loves listening to music, creating art, reading books, and visiting various local libraries for continued inspiration.